D1277734

Friendship

by Isaac Seder

Raintree

Chicago, Illinois

© 2004 Raintree

Published by Raintree, a division of Reed Elsevier, Inc.
Chicago, Illinois
Customer Service 888-363-4266
Visit our website at www.raintreelibrary.com

For information, address the publisher: Raintree, 100 N. LaSalle, Suite 1200, Chicago, IL 60602

Printed and bound in the United States by Lake Book Manufacturing, Inc.

08 07 06

10 9 8 7 6 5 4 3 2

Library of Congress Cataloging-in-Publication Data

Seder, Isaac.
    Friendship / Isaac Seder.
        p. cm. — (Character education)
Includes bibliographical references and index.
Contents: What is a friend? — The heart of a friend — Being there for your friends — New fun with old friends — All-weather friendships — When friends fight — How to make new friends — What do you look for in a friend? — Being yourself — Making your own choices — Finding friends in unlikely places — Friends who have not met — A hard thing to explain.
        ISBN 978-0-7398-7005-1 (0-7398-7005-X) (HC) ISBN 978-1-4109-0324-2 (1-4109-0324-9) (Pbk)
        1. Friendship — Juvenile literature. [1. Friendship.] I. Title. II. Series:
Character education (Raintree (Firm))
    BJ1533.F8S39 2003
    177'.62 — dc21
                                                                                            2003005897

A Creative Media Applications, Inc. Production
WRITER: Isaac Seder
DESIGN AND PRODUCTION: Alan Barnett, Inc.
EDITOR: Susan Madoff
COPYEDITOR: Laurie Lieb

Some words are shown in bold, **like this.** You can find what they mean by looking in the glossary.

Contents

"Of all possessions a friend is the most precious."

—Greek historian Herodotus

Some things have not changed very much since Herodotus wrote about friends more than 2,000 years ago. A good friend is still someone very special. Friends can share jokes, games, or secrets. Even a chore like cleaning your room can be fun when a friend helps you do it.

Friendship is a relationship between two or more people who like each other. You can build strong, lasting friendships by paying attention to how you treat other people. This book will give you some tips on how you can make and keep good friends.

Good friendships do not just happen. First, you have to take time to get to know someone. Once you are friends, your positive attitude and interest will help you build a strong friendship.

Of course, being a friend is not only about having fun and playing. Friends sometimes fight. They also can feel jealous of each other. They can hurt each other's feelings. Even so, good friends can get through tough times and still stay friends.

Sharing good times together is one of the best parts of a great friendship.

These boys live near each other in New York's South Bronx neighborhood. Their strong friendship is based on reliability, responsibility, and loyalty to each other.

Every friendship is different, but good friends all share some of the same qualities. Here is how some friends display the **values** that make their friendship strong.

Carmen is loyal to her friends. She is a friend to them no matter what happens. Loyalty is being faithful to other people.

When Mai says she will help her friend Susan with their homework, she does. **Reliability** means that friends can be trusted to do what is expected of them. Mai is a reliable friend because she does what she promises to do.

Rick has family chores to do on Saturdays. Even though he would rather play with his friend Paulo, he does not try to get out of his work. **Responsibility** is accepting your duties and being in control of your choices.

Paulo sometimes gets frustrated because Rick cannot play on Saturdays, but he never gives Rick a hard time about it. Paulo respects Rick and his family. **Respect** means having high regard for someone or something. You show your respect for people when you accept their habits, needs, and choices.

Emerson on friendship

In 1841 Ralph Waldo Emerson wrote about friendship. Throughout his life Emerson celebrated the joys of connecting with a close friend. He was writing partly about his good friend Henry David Thoreau. Together, Emerson and Thoreau wrote some of the most thoughtful essays in American literature.

Here are a few of Emerson's ideas about friendship. Some of the language has changed over the years, but the feelings are still true today.

- "The only way to have a friend is to be one."

- "A friend is a person with whom I may be sincere. Before him, I may think aloud."

- "Go oft [often] to the house of thy friend, for weeds choke the unused path."

Ralph Waldo Emerson understood the power of friendship and how it can enrich our lives.

Being There for Your Friends

Good friends can lean on each other for support or lend a helping hand.

Amelia Fitch, a fourth-grader who lives in Concord, Massachusetts, says that good friends should be there for each other. What does it mean to "be there" for a friend? Amelia explains that "being there means you know you can count on your friend no matter what. Friends share. Nobody hogs everything. Even when you're talking, you take turns."

Amelia's comment highlights two important parts of being a good friend—being supportive and listening. She knows that friends need to provide support, or help, for each other.

Friends support each other all the time, whether they are feeling happy, frustrated, angry, or sad. If your friend is excited about writing a poem, you can be supportive by reading the poem and making encouraging comments.

If your friend is having trouble with a math problem, you can be supportive by reviewing the homework together.

Listening to each other is another important part of being friends. Good friendships are balanced. Each friend contributes to every conversation, game, or activity.

Listen carefully to what your friends say. Sometimes, your friends might tell you something **in confidence.** That means they want you to keep this information private. Loyal friends know they can share anything.

In 1947 Pee Wee Reese was there for his friend Jackie Robinson. Robinson faced the hatred of many fans because he was the first African-American baseball player in the major leagues. Reese literally stood next to Robinson to show his support.

New Fun with Old Friends

You probably share a lot of things with your friends. Maybe you share similar interests—you like the same music, collect the same things, or like the same activities. However, when you spend a lot of time together, doing the same thing every time can get boring.

Trying new activities is a great way to build strong friendships. You and your friend will share interesting new experiences. You will have more to talk about and more in common.

Working together on things you enjoy can help build strong friendships.

New activities also can balance a friendship. Matt and Koji are friends, but Koji has been playing tennis for three years while Matt has been playing only for a few months. When they play together, Matt gets frustrated because he always loses the game. The boys decide to take swimming lessons together. Since neither of them is a very good swimmer, they start the lessons at the same level.

Sometimes trying new things can be scary. Having a friend there with you can help you feel more confident.

Here are some other activities that can bring new ideas and energy to your friendships.

- Volunteer together. Look for places you can help out in your community. You might visit a retirement home or a hospital together.

- Read the same books. You will always have something new to talk about when you both finish reading the book.

- Start your own project together. You might start a dog-walking service or build a clubhouse. A good project might keep going for a month or more. It will give you something to look forward to doing with your friends.

Adam's friend Jason has one annoying habit. Every time Adam asks for help, Jason is busy. If Adam needs help with his homework, Jason is nowhere to be found. When Adam is sick, Jason is too busy to visit him. But when Adam is free for a ball game or to go for ice cream, Jason is right by his side.

Many people might call Jason a "fair-weather friend." He is a good friend when things are going well. But when things get tough, Jason does not act like a friend.

Good friends are better than that. They stick by each other all the time, not just when it is fun. Remember the golden rule—treat others the way you would like to be treated. That rule goes double for friends.

According to the reporter Walter Winchell, "A friend is one who walks in when the rest of the world walks out." A true friend can help you face situations that might seem impossible.

Brian Piccolo and Gale Sayers became friends when they played football for the Chicago Bears. Their friendship has become famous for the way they helped each other face tough times. When Sayers injured himself, Piccolo helped him stick to a hard recovery plan.

Then Piccolo developed cancer. Sayers proved that he was truly a friend for all seasons. He did not run away from the bad news. He stayed to help his friend.

Two television movies have been made celebrating the friendship between Gayle Sayers (left) and Brian Piccolo. Both versions of "Brian's Song" (1971 and 2001) celebrate the power of a supportive friendship.

When Friends Fight

Alana and Dory are planning a picnic for their families. They are having fun until Alana says she wants to make mini-meatballs. Dory screams in frustration. "I'm a vegetarian," she shouts. "You never listen to me because you're stuck up." All of a sudden, the two friends are shouting at each other. Alana stomps out the door, yelling "I'm not coming to your stupid picnic!"

Disagreements are part of every friendship. But Alana and Dory are not managing their differences very well. Good friends can learn to stay polite and calm even when they do not agree. Your chances of resolving an argument are much greater if you quietly listen to each other's opinions and pay attention to each other's needs.

Fighting fair

These tips can help solve problems between friends.

- **Stay calm.** Even if you are full of energy, try to express yourself without anger. If you start shouting, your friend is sure to join in. Getting loud will not solve anything. If you find that you cannot control your anger, it is a good idea to take a break from your friend and return to talk about things when you've calmed down.

Before you get too angry, try taking a break. Just step back and do not say anything for a moment. Pausing to think can help you stay calm and avoid big fights.

- **Be a good listener.** Do not interrupt when your friend is talking. Make sure you understand what your friend is saying. If you do not understand something, just ask.

- **Be polite.** Instead of saying "There is no way I will go to that rotten movie with you," try something more polite. It is better to say, "I really don't think I would like that movie. Maybe there is something playing that we both want to see."

- **Offer suggestions.** Look for solutions that will satisfy both of you. A compromise is a solution in which both people give up some part of what they want. If you want to play basketball and your friend wants to listen to a new CD, you might compromise by spending a half-hour doing each activity.

How to Make New Friends

Babe Didrikson Zaharias was a famous all-around athlete, winning competitions as a runner, basketball player, and swimmer. But her many awards were not the most important thing in her life. "Winning has always

If you are thrown into a new situation, it's natural to feel a little shy. Give yourself time to meet your new classmates and neighbors. Friendships will develop gradually.

Making New Friends

Follow these hints when you meet new people:

- **Ask questions.** You can break the ice by asking people about their interests.

- **Keep eye contact.** When you talk to people, give them your full attention by looking at them.

- **Remember names.** If you have trouble remembering people's names, try repeating the name a few times after you meet them. If someone says, "My name is Jiwan," say "Hi, Jiwan." You also might ask how to spell the name.

- **Keep an open mind.** When you are meeting people, never make assumptions based on how they look. That is called **prejudice,** and it is not a fair way to treat people. It also can keep you from getting to know someone who might be a terrific friend.

meant much to me," she said, "but winning friends has meant the most."

Winning friends takes time. You need to get to know someone before you become good friends.

It is natural to feel shy when you meet people for the first time. Remember that they are probably feeling the same way.

What Do You Look for in a Friend?

Why do some people become friends and some do not? Friends usually share some of the same interests, habits, and values. You will not share these things with everyone.

That does not mean that friends are exactly like each other. Your friends may not look the same or act like you at all. What matters is that you enjoy being together and that you support each other.

When Jorge describes his friend Neil, you notice at once that the two friends share some traits, but not

You usually cannot tell why people are friends just by looking at them. Friends share qualities that are beneath the surface.

What Is Important to You: A Checklist

Look at this list of qualities. Which one is most important to you in a friend? Which ones do not matter very much at all? Rank the qualities as very important (VI), important (I), or not important (NI).

____ sense of humor

____ kindness

____ personal appearance

____ popularity

____ lives nearby

____ intelligence

____ same interests

____ ability to keep a secret

____ values and religious beliefs

____ loyalty

others. "Neil is much funnier than I am. He is always making up jokes and making me laugh. We both think the same things are funny. I am more **responsible** than Neil. Whenever we play together, I am the one who watches the time. Otherwise we would miss dinner."

When you are meeting new people, take time to decide whether or not you want to become friends. Use the checklist on this page to help you think about what you want in a friend. Choosing your friends is an important step. As Benjamin Franklin said, "Be slow in choosing a friend, slower in changing."

Being Yourself

What do you see when you look in a mirror? You should see a unique person who enjoys being you.

Your friends should like you for who you are. Sometimes it is tempting to pretend to be someone else in order to fit in. You might pretend to like something that does not interest you. Or you might pretend that you are skillful in a sport or a craft, even though you're really not.

Nate is eager to make friends at his new school. When two of his classmates ask him to go ice-skating on Saturday, Nate does not want to admit that he has never ice-skated. He says that he left his skates at his old house and is getting a new pair for his birthday next month. Now Nate is worried about what will happen when his new friends find out he really cannot skate at all.

Nate forgot one of the most important rules about making friends: Always be true to yourself. If you lie about who you are, people will never really know you. You also might get trapped in awkward situations, like Nate and his ice skates.

Instead of pretending he knew how to skate, Nate could have asked questions about how to learn to skate or which brand of equipment is best. Nate assumed that his new classmates would not like him if he told the truth, but the opposite is more likely to be true. People respond positively to someone who seems honest and **genuine.**

When you show that you are proud of who you are, you show **self-confidence.** Respect yourself, and other people are bound to follow.

What Do You Like?

What are some of the similarities and differences between you and your friends?

- Do you listen to the same music or do your tastes differ?

- Do you play the same sports? Do you play on different teams? Do you each have a different sport in which you excel?

- How do you and your friends handle disagreements?

- Do you and your friends enjoy the same classes in school or are you interested in different subjects?

Making Your Own Choices

A big part of being yourself is recognizing your **values** and sticking to them. Your values are the ideas and beliefs that are important to you. You might place a high value on honesty and fair play. You also might value a sense of humor and a positive way of looking at things.

Your values should not change with your friends. Sometimes you might be tempted to act against your values to fit in with a group. If you value health and a strong body, you know that smoking goes against your values. Yet you might be tempted to start smoking to fit in with a cool group of kids. But as General Robert E. Lee once said, "Never do a wrong thing to make a friend or keep one."

Peer pressure is social pressure to do something in order to be accepted by others. Remember that every decision you make reflects on you and your values. If you do something that goes against your values, you are presenting yourself dishonestly. If you give in to peer pressure, you may end up feeling bad about yourself and your actions.

Of course, some peer pressure is not of real importance. If a group is wearing red T-shirts during gym class, you can probably become part of this trend without going against any of your values.

Students in schools sometimes form **cliques**—close groups of friends who try to keep out other people. A clique often emphasizes negative relationships—the members spend a lot of time thinking about who does not belong. Cliques keep other people out to make their members feel special. Before you become part of a clique, think carefully about your decision. Make sure that the people in the clique will respect your right to make your own choices.

Some friends form cliques that focus on being as alike as possible. These friendships can be difficult because you may find it hard to be yourself.

Finding Friends in Unlikely Places

Good friendships usually grow slowly. They become stronger as you get to know someone better. When you are making new friends, allow plenty of time to really get to know someone.

Friendships might begin where you least expect them. There might be someone at school who teases you or gives you a hard time. Or maybe you have a **rivalry**—an ongoing competition—with another student who plays your favorite sport.

Basketball greats Magic Johnson and Larry Bird were fierce rivals on the court. From this unlikely starting place, the two athletes grew to become off-court friends.

You might think there is no way you can be friends with people like that. Actually, one of the best ways to handle people who seem to be unlikely friends is to invite them to your house for a meal or to go with your family to a movie. Meeting away from school, you might find that you have plenty of things in common. You might even become good friends.

Although Anne Sullivan began as Helen Keller's teacher, she soon became her closest friend.

Helen Keller became blind and deaf when she was two years old. When she was seven, Anne Sullivan became her teacher. At first Helen felt angry with Anne because Anne made Helen work hard and wouldn't put up with Helen's spoiled ways. Anne kept trying to teach Helen to communicate. From this shaky beginning, Helen and Anne formed a powerful lifelong friendship.

Friends Who Have Not Met

One of the newest ways you might find a friend is by using your computer. More and more children around the world are making friends through the Internet. Key pals are friends who write to each other by e-mail.

Exchanging information with friends online can help you understand other cultures. Close friendships can develop as you get to know each other through your writing. Sometimes it can be easier to share your thoughts

Your computer can help you meet friends across the country or around the world.

by writing than by speaking. Your teacher or librarian can help you find Internet sites where children can meet.

Unusual projects can give key pals a fun way to get to know each other. Students at Freemont Magnet Elementary School have shared many experiences with key pals. In one class project, students pooled their information to compare the prices of toys, groceries, and fast food in Australia, Italy, Finland, England, Ireland, and the United States. In another project, friends mailed written descriptions of themselves, and their key pals created drawings based on their descriptions.

Being safe online

When you make friends online, you need to follow some rules to protect your safety.

- Never tell your full name. Only tell your first name or your online ID.

- Do not give out any personal information, such as your address, telephone number, parents' names, or your Social Security number.

- Never agree to meet with someone you met online. If you want to arrange a meeting, ask an adult for help.

- Tell your parents or a teacher if anyone writes an inappropriate message to you.

- Do not send pictures of yourself.

Muhammad Ali, a champion boxer, once summed up his feelings about friendship. He said, "Friendship is the hardest thing in the world to explain. It is not something you learn in school. But if you have not learned the meaning of friendship, you really have not learned anything."

Every friendship is as unique as the people in it. Your friendships reflect the things that make you special.

You and your friends can enjoy many activities together. Your friendships will grow stronger with each hour you spend together.

Ben Cohen and Jerry Greenfield, founders of Ben & Jerry's ice cream company, became friends in seventh grade.

Friends have fun together, but they also help each other and care about each other. The more you know about your friends, the stronger your friendships will be. Try interviewing your friend. You might pretend you are a reporter from a TV show. Ask your friend different questions. Ask about likes and dislikes and feelings about important topics and events. Your friend's answers might surprise you. They will certainly help you get to know your friend in new ways.

Loyalty, **responsibility,** and honesty are big parts of a good friendship. Treat your friends the way you would like to be treated. You are lucky to have your friends, and they are lucky to have you!

Glossary

clique close groups of friends who try to keep out other people

genuine real, honest, and open with others

in confidence something that is meant to be kept private

peer pressure social pressure to do something to be accepted by a person or group

prejudice making assumptions or judgments about people based on what they look like or how they seem at first

reliability being able to be trusted to do what is expected of you

respect high regard or esteem for someone or something

responsibility accepting your duties and being in control of your choices

rivalry ongoing competition

self-confidence showing that you are proud of who you are

values ideas and beliefs that are important to you

Naylor, Phyllis Reynolds. *Getting Along with Your Friends.* Nashville: Abingdon, 1980.

The author of many popular books and articles for young readers gives helpful advice for building strong friendships.

Paterson, Katherine. *Bridge to Terabithia.* New York: Scholastic, 1993.

A surprising and touching friendship develops when Jess and Leslie both want to become the fastest runner in fifth grade.

Philbrick, Rodman. *Freak the Mighty.* New York: Scholastic, 1993.

This exciting novel describes the unlikely friendship that develops between a brilliant young man and a student with learning disabilities.

Index